TEXAS TEST PREP
Practice Test Book
STAAR Reading
Grade 4

© 2011 by Test Master Press

All rights reserved. No part of this book may be reproduced or transmitted in any form or by any means, electronic, mechanical, photocopying, recording, or otherwise without prior written permission.

ISBN 978-1466374430

CONTENTS

Section 1: Reading Mini-Tests	4
Introduction to the Reading Mini-Tests	5
STAAR Reading Mini-Test 1	6
STAAR Reading Mini-Test 2	13
STAAR Reading Mini-Test 3	19
STAAR Reading Mini-Test 4	25
STAAR Reading Mini-Test 5	31
STAAR Reading Mini-Test 6	38
STAAR Reading Mini-Test 7	44
STAAR Reading Mini-Test 8	51
Section 2: Vocabulary Quizzes	58
Introduction to the Vocabulary Quizzes	59
Quiz 1: Identify Word Meanings	60
Quiz 2: Analyze Word Meanings	62
Quiz 3: Use Synonyms and Antonyms	64
Quiz 4: Use Prefixes	66
Quiz 5: Use Suffixes	68
Quiz 6: Use Greek and Latin Roots	70
Section 3: STAAR Reading Practice Test	72
Introduction to the Reading Practice Test	73
STAAR Reading Practice Test	74
Answer Key	107
Section 1: Reading Mini-Tests	108
Section 2: Vocabulary Quizzes	117
Section 3: STAAR Reading Practice Test	119
Multiple Choice Answer Sheet	126

Section 1
Reading Mini-Tests

INTRODUCTION TO THE READING MINI-TESTS
For Parents, Teachers, and Tutors

How Reading is Assessed by the State of Texas

The STAAR Reading test assesses reading skills by having students read passages and answer reading comprehension questions about the passages. On the STAAR Reading test, students read 6 to 7 passages and answer a total of 44 multiple-choice questions.

About the Reading Mini-Tests

This section of the practice test book contains passages and question sets similar to those on the STAAR Reading tests. However, students can take mini-tests instead of taking a complete practice test. Each mini-test has one passage for students to read. Students then answer 8 multiple-choice questions about the passage.

This section of the book is an effective way for students to build up to taking the full-length test. Students can focus on one passage and a small set of questions at a time. This will build confidence and help students become familiar with answering test questions. Students will gradually develop the skills they need to complete the full-length practice test in Section 3 of this book.

Reading Skills

The STAAR Reading test given by the state of Texas tests a specific set of skills. The full answer key at the end of the book identifies what skill each question is testing.

There are also key reading skills that students will need to understand to master the STAAR Reading test. The answer key includes additional information on these key skills so you can help the student gain understanding.

STAAR Reading

Mini-Test 1

> **Instructions**
>
> Read the passage. The passage is followed by questions.
>
> Read each question carefully. Then select the best answer. Fill in the circle for the correct answer.

The Change

Maria was a beautiful young girl. She had long flowing blond hair and stunning blue eyes. Maria was still very <u>insecure</u> about her appearance. She often thought that most of her friends were prettier than her. One day a new girl joined her school. Her name was Sarah. Sarah had <u>dark</u> brown hair and emerald green eyes. Maria wished she looked like her new friend. Over time she became jealous of Sarah. One day she decided to take action.

She thought that if she looked like Sarah then she would feel much better. So she took her allowance money and headed to the mall with her older sister Bronwyn. She visited a hair salon and purchased some colored hair dye. When she returned home, she told her mother what she planned to do.

"It's your decision," said her mother sadly. "But I think you look beautiful as you are."

Maria ignored her mother's words and headed to the bathroom. She spent several hours dying her hair dark brown. She felt much better and <u>skipped</u> her way into school the following day. As she reached her class she noticed a new blond girl sitting near the front. She realized that it was Sarah. Her friend had dyed her hair a lighter shade of blond. It was almost identical to how Maria's had looked before. Sarah turned around and Maria spoke to her.

"Why did you dye your hair?" Maria asked.

Sarah paused.

"Well, I always loved your hair," Sarah replied. "I thought it would be cool if we matched."

Maria slumped in her chair and sighed.

1   Read this sentence from the passage.

Maria was still very <u>insecure</u> about her appearance.

If the word <u>secure</u> means "confident," what does the word <u>insecure</u> mean?

Ⓐ   More confident

Ⓑ   Less confident

Ⓒ   Not confident

Ⓓ   Most confident

2   Read this sentence from the passage.

Sarah had <u>dark</u> brown hair and emerald green eyes.

Which word means the opposite of <u>dark</u>?

Ⓐ   Short

Ⓑ   Light

Ⓒ   Deep

Ⓓ   Bright

3 Who is the main character in the passage?

- Ⓐ Sarah
- Ⓑ Maria's mother
- Ⓒ Maria
- Ⓓ Bronwyn

4 Read this sentence from the passage.

> **She felt much better and <u>skipped</u> her way into school the following day.**

What does the word <u>skipped</u> suggest about Maria?

- Ⓐ She felt nervous.
- Ⓑ She was happy.
- Ⓒ She moved quietly.
- Ⓓ She was running late.

5 Who is telling the story?

- Ⓐ Sarah
- Ⓑ Maria
- Ⓒ Maria's mother
- Ⓓ Someone not in the story

6 What is Maria's main problem in the passage?

- Ⓐ She does not feel good about her looks.
- Ⓑ She does not have enough friends.
- Ⓒ She has never dyed her hair before.
- Ⓓ She wants Sarah to like her.

7 What does Maria do right after she gets home from the mall?

- Ⓐ She asks her sister to help her dye her hair.
- Ⓑ She tells her mother she is going to dye her hair.
- Ⓒ She learns that Sarah is also dying her hair.
- Ⓓ She goes to the bathroom to dye her hair.

8 What is the main message of the passage?

Ⓐ　Talk about your problems.

Ⓑ　Be willing to change.

Ⓒ　Listen to the people around you.

Ⓓ　Be happy with who you are.

STAAR Reading

Mini-Test 2

Instructions

Read the passage. The passage is followed by questions.

Read each question carefully. Then select the best answer. Fill in the circle for the correct answer.

Muhammad Ali

Muhammad Ali is a famous American boxer. He was born in 1942. Many people believe that he is the greatest boxer of all time. Ali won the World Heavyweight Championship three times. He fought on four different continents. He had his first success as an amateur boxer. In 1960, he won an Olympic gold medal. During this time, he was known as Cassius Clay. He changed his name in 1964.

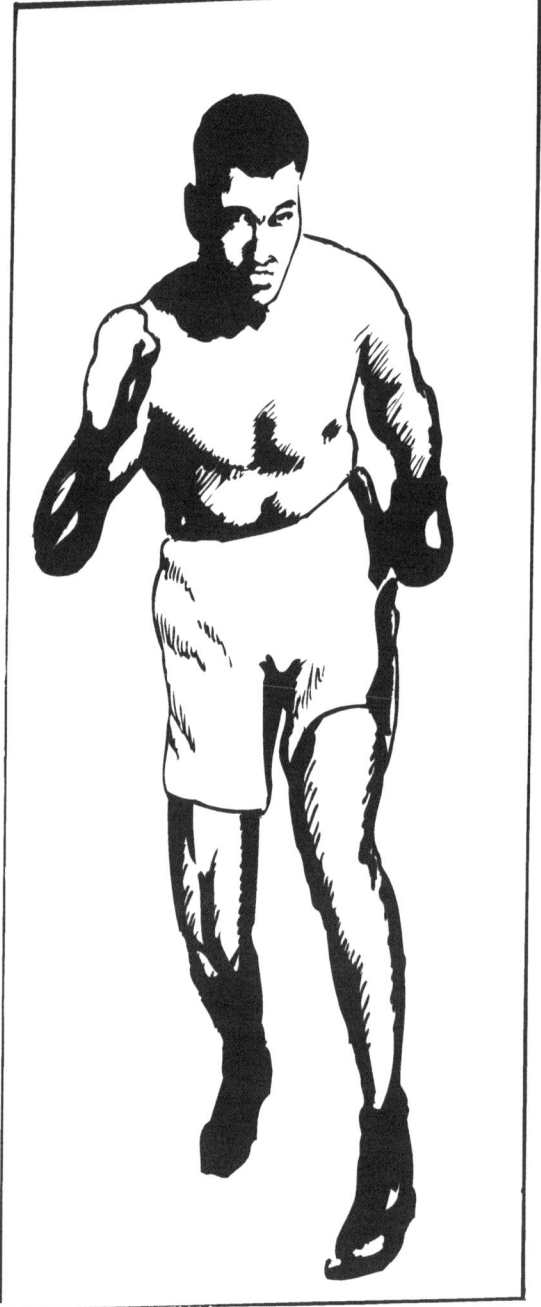

Ali became known as a fast and <u>powerful</u> fighter. He was also very confident. He often predicted which round he would win each fight. He won his first title in 1964 after beating the fearsome Sonny Liston. Ali defended his title several times. By 1967, he was considered to be unbeatable. Then the Vietnam War occurred. Ali was meant to go to war, but he refused. He was stripped of his title. He was arrested and had his boxing license taken away. He fought the charges. He won his right to freedom. He also won the right to box again. In 1971, he continued his career.

He had lost some of his speed and power. However, he still <u>reclaimed</u> his title twice. He had famous bouts with Joe Frazier and George Foreman. He won both of these fights. His last fight was against Trevor Berbick in 1981. He was not as quick as usual, and he lost the fight.

He retired with a career record of 56 wins and 5 defeats. Ali now spends much of his time working with charities. In 1996, the Olympics were held in Atlanta. Ali was chosen to light the torch. It was a great way to honor a great sportsman.

1   Read this sentence from the passage.

   Ali became known as a fast and powerful fighter.

   Which word means about the same as powerful?

   Ⓐ   Angry

   Ⓑ   Quick

   Ⓒ   Skilled

   Ⓓ   Strong

2   In the third paragraph, what does the word reclaimed mean?

   Ⓐ   Less claimed

   Ⓑ   Not claimed

   Ⓒ   Claimed again

   Ⓓ   Claimed before

Grade 4 Practice Test Book

3 Who did Ali defeat to win his first boxing title?

- Ⓐ Sonny Liston
- Ⓑ Joe Frazier
- Ⓒ George Foreman
- Ⓓ Trevor Berbick

4 The passage is most like –

- Ⓐ a biography
- Ⓑ an advertisement
- Ⓒ a short story
- Ⓓ a news article

5 Which detail from the passage is least important?

- Ⓐ Ali is thought of as the greatest boxer of all time.
- Ⓑ Ali fought on four different continents.
- Ⓒ Ali won his first world title in 1964.
- Ⓓ Ali had 56 wins and 5 defeats.

6 Which sentence from the passage is an opinion?

- Ⓐ *In 1960, he won an Olympic gold medal.*
- Ⓑ *During this time, he was known as Cassius Clay.*
- Ⓒ *His last fight was against Trevor Berbick in 1981.*
- Ⓓ *It was a great way to honor a great sportsman.*

7 Which sentence from the passage best supports the idea that Ali was a successful boxer?

- Ⓐ *Ali won the World Heavyweight Championship three times.*
- Ⓑ *During this time, he was known as Cassius Clay.*
- Ⓒ *He often predicted which round he would win each fight.*
- Ⓓ *He also won the right to box again.*

8 How is the passage mainly organized?

- Ⓐ A problem is described and then a solution is given.
- Ⓑ Events are described in the order they occurred.
- Ⓒ Facts are given to support an argument.
- Ⓓ A question is asked and then answered.

STAAR Reading

Mini-Test 3

Instructions

Read the passage. The passage is followed by questions.

Read each question carefully. Then select the best answer. Fill in the circle for the correct answer.

Little Things
by Ebenezer Cobham Brewer

Little drops of water,
Little grains of sand,
Make the <u>mighty</u> ocean
And the pleasant land.

Thus the little minutes,
Humble though they be,
Make the mighty ages
Of <u>eternity</u>.

1   Read these lines from the poem.

> **Make the mighty ages**
> **Of <u>eternity</u>.**

What does the word <u>eternity</u> most likely mean?

- Ⓐ   Time
- Ⓑ   Forever
- Ⓒ   Earth
- Ⓓ   Everything

2   Read this line from the poem.

> **Make the <u>mighty</u> ocean**

The word <u>mighty</u> suggests that the ocean is –

- Ⓐ   strange
- Ⓑ   scary
- Ⓒ   powerful
- Ⓓ   small

3 Which word best describes the mood of the poem?

- Ⓐ Gloomy
- Ⓑ Scary
- Ⓒ Tired
- Ⓓ Cheerful

4 Read this line from the poem.

Make the mighty ages

Which literary technique does the author use in this line?

- Ⓐ Alliteration
- Ⓑ Simile
- Ⓒ Metaphor
- Ⓓ Flashback

5 What is the rhyme pattern of each stanza of the poem?

- Ⓐ All the lines rhyme with each other.
- Ⓑ There are two pairs of rhyming lines.
- Ⓒ The second and fourth lines rhyme.
- Ⓓ None of the lines rhyme.

6 Which word is repeated in the poem?

- Ⓐ *little*
- Ⓑ *drops*
- Ⓒ *ocean*
- Ⓓ *ages*

7 What is the main idea of the poem?

- Ⓐ Little things can form great things.
- Ⓑ Everything is always changing.
- Ⓒ Life could not survive without water.
- Ⓓ Time can go fast or slow.

8 What is the second stanza about?

- Ⓐ Nature
- Ⓑ Earth
- Ⓒ Time
- Ⓓ Sleep

STAAR Reading

Mini-Test 4

Instructions

Read the passage. The passage is followed by questions.

Read each question carefully. Then select the best answer. Fill in the circle for the correct answer.

Grooming a King Charles Cavalier

The King Charles Cavalier is a small breed of Spaniel dog. It is known as a toy dog by kennel clubs. They are very popular in the United States and around the world. These dogs have a <u>silky</u> coat and can be difficult to groom. Professional groomers can carry out the task. However, many owners choose to save money and groom their dog themselves.

Start by making sure you have the correct equipment to groom your dog correctly. You will need:
- a comb
- a brush
- dog-friendly conditioner

Step 1
Before you start, make sure that your dog is in a comfortable position either on your lap or on a blanket.

Step 2
Take your comb and move it smoothly through their coat. Be <u>gentle</u> and make sure that all dead or matted hair is removed.

Step 3
Once the combing is complete, add some of the conditioner to the coat. This will add shine and make it easier to brush your dog.

Step 4
Comb your dog's coat for a second time to make sure that it is as smooth as it can be.

Step 5
It is now time to brush your King Charles Cavalier. Hold the brush firmly in your hand and be sure to keep your dog still. Move the brush gently through your dog's coat. Take care to smooth out any lumps or patches of uneven hair. Move through each area of the coat twice.

Step 6
Once you've finished brushing, condition your dogs coat again. This helps to keep your dog's coat free from tangles. It will also make it easier to groom your dog in the future.

Step 7
Lastly, all you need to do is rinse the dog's coat and gently pat it dry.

1   Read this sentence from the passage.

> **Be gentle and make sure that all dead or matted hair is removed.**

Which word means the opposite of gentle?

- Ⓐ   Calm
- Ⓑ   Fast
- Ⓒ   Rough
- Ⓓ   Slow

2   Read this sentence from the passage.

> **These dogs have a silky coat and can be difficult to groom.**

What does the word silky mainly describe?

- Ⓐ   How long the coat is
- Ⓑ   How the coat feels
- Ⓒ   What the coat smells like
- Ⓓ   What color the coat is

3 Which of these is NOT a reason for adding conditioner?

- Ⓐ To add shine to the coat
- Ⓑ To stop the coat from getting tangles
- Ⓒ To prevent the dog from getting fleas
- Ⓓ To make it easier to brush the dog

4 What is the main purpose of the passage?

- Ⓐ To teach readers how to do something
- Ⓑ To entertain readers with a story
- Ⓒ To inform readers about a type of dog
- Ⓓ To compare different types of dog products

5 What is the purpose of the bullet points?

- Ⓐ To describe the steps
- Ⓑ To give hints and tips
- Ⓒ To list the items needed
- Ⓓ To highlight the key points

6 In which step is the conditioner first needed?

- Ⓐ Step 1
- Ⓑ Step 3
- Ⓒ Step 5
- Ⓓ Step 7

7 Which detail from the picture is most relevant to the passage?

- Ⓐ The size of the dog
- Ⓑ The color of the dog
- Ⓒ The look of the dog's fur
- Ⓓ The look on the dog's face

8 According to the passage, what should you do right after brushing the dog?

- Ⓐ Comb the dog's coat a second time
- Ⓑ Condition the dog's coat
- Ⓒ Rinse the dog's coat
- Ⓓ Give the dog a treat

STAAR Reading

Mini-Test 5

Instructions

Read the passage. The passage is followed by questions.

Read each question carefully. Then select the best answer. Fill in the circle for the correct answer.

The Girlfriend and the Mother

Prince Arnold had a very close <u>bond</u> with his mother. They shared everything with each other. They had remained close since he had been a child. One day, he met a girl named Chloe. They soon became boyfriend and girlfriend. Gradually, Arnold began to spend more time with his girlfriend than he did with his mother. Although he still enjoyed long conversations with his mother, she began to feel left out. She felt that the only time she would get to spend with him was in the evenings. This was when he would fall asleep on the couch and she would sit beside him and stroke his hair.

His mother really liked the gray strands that grew in his hair. She felt they made him look wise. So as she stroked his head she would remove some of the darker hairs from his scalp. She did this over many nights for an entire year.

Arnold's girlfriend had a similar habit. She thought that his gray hairs made him look old. So she would pluck as many gray hairs from his head as she possibly could. She too did this for many nights over the year.

After a year had gone by, Arnold found that he was completely bald. His mother and girlfriend had <u>removed</u> all of his hair. Both women and Arnold were unhappy with his new look. The ladies felt that their battle for his time had led to the problem.

"We're so sorry," they said. "What we have done is unfair."

They realized that they must all get along and spend time together if they were to remain happy. The mother and the girlfriend made a promise to be happy sharing Prince Arnold's time.

1   Read this sentence from the passage.

> **His mother and girlfriend had <u>removed</u> all of his hair.**

What does the word <u>removed</u> mean?

- Ⓐ   Scared off
- Ⓑ   Fought over
- Ⓒ   Taken away
- Ⓓ   Changed places

2   Read this sentence from the passage.

> **Prince Arnold had a very close <u>bond</u> with his mother.**

Which meaning of the word <u>bond</u> is used in the sentence?

- Ⓐ   To connect two or more items
- Ⓑ   A relationship or link between people
- Ⓒ   An agreement or promise
- Ⓓ   A type of glue

3   What is the mother's main problem in the passage?

   Ⓐ   She dislikes her son's hair.

   Ⓑ   She does not want to share her son.

   Ⓒ   She argues with her son.

   Ⓓ   She wants her son to get married.

4   "The Girlfriend and the Mother" is most like a —

   Ⓐ   true story

   Ⓑ   science fiction story

   Ⓒ   biography

   Ⓓ   fable

5   How are the girlfriend and the mother alike?

   Ⓐ   They are both pleased when Arnold is bald.

   Ⓑ   They both pluck out Arnold's hair.

   Ⓒ   They both dislike Arnold's gray hair.

   Ⓓ   They have both known Arnold since he was young.

6   How does the mother change in the passage?

   Ⓐ   She realizes that her son is a grown man.

   Ⓑ   She accepts her son and Chloe's relationship.

   Ⓒ   She loses interest in her son.

   Ⓓ   She learns that Chloe is a nice person.

7   According to the passage, Chloe thinks that Arnold's gray hair makes him look –

   Ⓐ   wise

   Ⓑ   royal

   Ⓒ   old

   Ⓓ   kind

8   What will the mother most likely do next?

   Ⓐ   Come up with a plan to break up her son and Chloe

   Ⓑ   Start making an effort to spend time with her son and Chloe

   Ⓒ   Make her son think that his baldness is Chloe's fault

   Ⓓ   Start spending time with her husband instead of her son

STAAR Reading

Mini-Test 6

Instructions

Read the passage. The passage is followed by questions.

Read each question carefully. Then select the best answer. Fill in the circle for the correct answer.

Moving On

March 13, 2011

Dear Sirs:

I hope this letter finds you well. I am writing to let you know that I wish to resign from my <u>position</u>. It is my plan to leave after working my 3-month notice period. As you are aware, I was planning to move my family to Florida in 6 months time. I have since decided to move sooner. I hope this does not cause you too many problems. I am happy to assist in training a replacement during this time.

I have enjoyed my 6 years with the company. I am also <u>grateful</u> for the time you took to train and develop my skills. I am sure you will understand my need to move on. My wife has been offered an excellent job in Florida. We have agreed to move as a family. With two young children, I did not want us to be separated because of work. We are planning to start moving into our new house at the start of June.

I am happy to discuss this further with you in person. I will return to work on Monday, June 20th after my current vacation in Texas. We can then sit down and work out the details. If you have any questions, please call my cell or feel free to email me. Once again, I would like to thank you for your understanding. I also thank you for the help that you have given me in my career. I hope that our paths cross again in the future.

Yours faithfully,

Lucas Dutton

1	Read this sentence from the letter.

>	**I am also <u>grateful</u> for the time you took to train and develop my skills.**

Which word means about the same as <u>grateful</u>?

Ⓐ	Thoughtful

Ⓑ	Hurtful

Ⓒ	Hateful

Ⓓ	Thankful

2	Which meaning of the word <u>position</u> is used in the first paragraph?

Ⓐ	A location

Ⓑ	A job

Ⓒ	A situation

Ⓓ	A rank

3 According to the letter, where is Lucas moving to?

Ⓐ New York

Ⓑ Texas

Ⓒ Florida

Ⓓ California

4 What is the main reason Lucas wrote the letter?

Ⓐ To tell where he is moving to

Ⓑ To explain that he is leaving

Ⓒ To show how much he enjoyed his work

Ⓓ To stop his bosses from worrying about him

5 What is the main reason that Lucas is leaving his job sooner than he expected?

Ⓐ His wife has found a job in Florida.

Ⓑ His wife is having another child.

Ⓒ He no longer likes his job.

Ⓓ He is enjoying his vacation too much.

6 Read this sentence from the letter.

I hope that our paths cross again in the future.

What does this sentence mean?

Ⓐ   I hope you are not angry.

Ⓑ   I hope that we meet again.

Ⓒ   I hope I move back one day.

Ⓓ   I hope you will remember me.

7 Which sentence best shows that Lucas is grateful to his employer?

Ⓐ   *I hope this does not cause you too many problems.*

Ⓑ   *I am sure you will understand my need to move on.*

Ⓒ   *If you have any questions, please call my cell or feel free to email me.*

Ⓓ   *I also thank you for the help that you have given me in my career.*

8 How does Lucas most likely feel about moving?

Ⓐ   Annoyed

Ⓑ   Sad

Ⓒ   Excited

Ⓓ   Worried

STAAR Reading

Mini-Test 7

Instructions

Read the passage. The passage is followed by questions.

Read each question carefully. Then select the best answer. Fill in the circle for the correct answer.

Catching Up

June 15, 2011

Dear Sally,

I really hope that this letter finds you well. I am writing to see how you are doing at college. Are you settling in well? I remember how upset you got when we dropped you off. I hate to think of you as being unhappy. I know what a bright and cheerful girl you are. It is hard to imagine you any other way! I am sure that you have already made a lot of new friends. How are your courses going? Are you enjoying the work and learning a lot? I bet you are finding it very interesting. I am so proud of you for studying and working your way toward your goals. It is motivating me in my own studies.

Everything is fine at home. I am halfway through my exams and have been enjoying them so far. I am <u>prepared</u> and relaxed when I attend each one. So far, they have all been a piece of cake. If all goes well, I may even be following in your footsteps in a few years time. We could even find ourselves at the same college. Having said that, I am not sure how much work we would actually get done! Knowing us we would either be having too much fun or wasting time with silly arguments. Seriously though, I really miss our chats and spending lots of time together.

Dad and Mom are great as always. Dad is due for a promotion at work and may even have to travel to London. Mom is trying to get fit for our summer vacation. I know you can't make it, but you will be <u>sorely</u> missed. I am hoping that you will be able to make it back next year to travel with us. Any trip abroad is just not the same without you!

Anyhow, I know you are working hard and that it is all for your future. So take care and I look forward to seeing you soon. Please write back to me when you get the chance. Until then, you will remain in my thoughts.

Lots of love,

Rory

1 Read this sentence from the passage.

> **I am prepared and relaxed when I attend each one.**

Which word could best be used in place of prepared?

Ⓐ   Calm

Ⓑ   Ready

Ⓒ   Studied

Ⓓ   Patient

2 Read this sentence from the passage.

> **I know you can't make it, but you will be sorely missed.**

As it is used in the sentence, what does sorely mean?

Ⓐ   Certainly

Ⓑ   Suddenly

Ⓒ   Sadly

Ⓓ   Greatly

3 Read this sentence from the passage.

> **So far, they have all been a piece of cake.**

The phrase "a piece of cake" means that something is –

- Ⓐ easy
- Ⓑ tasty
- Ⓒ quick
- Ⓓ funny

4 What is the second paragraph mostly about?

- Ⓐ What Rory has been doing at home
- Ⓑ What Rory imagines his sister is doing
- Ⓒ Why Rory misses his sister
- Ⓓ What Rory plans to do after school

5   How does Rory most likely feel about his sister not going on family vacations?

   Ⓐ   Pleased

   Ⓑ   Upset

   Ⓒ   Annoyed

   Ⓓ   Surprised

6   Rory would be most likely to say that he is –

   Ⓐ   embarrassed by Sally

   Ⓑ   proud of Sally

   Ⓒ   jealous of Sally

   Ⓓ   confused by Sally

7 Based on the passage, what can you conclude about Rory and Sally?

Ⓐ   They are very close.

Ⓑ   They want similar careers.

Ⓒ   They are the same age.

Ⓓ   They fight with each other a lot.

8 What type of passage is "Catching Up"?

Ⓐ   Short story

Ⓑ   Diary

Ⓒ   Letter

Ⓓ   Fable

STAAR Reading

Mini-Test 8

Instructions

Read the passage. The passage is followed by questions.

Read each question carefully. Then select the best answer. Fill in the circle for the correct answer.

The Shining Light Day Center

As parents, the wellbeing of your children is very important. It is important to keep them happy and healthy. It is also important to make sure they are active. It is especially important for children under the age of five. During this time, children learn quickly. They also develop skills <u>easier</u>. As parents, it can be hard to find time for all this. At the Shining Light Day Center, we understand this. We have created a range of activities to help your child.

Our activities cover many different areas. We want to help children think and learn. We want to help children learn to work with others. We want to help children learn to read and speak. We also want to help children be fit and healthy. Our activities include classes, games, and time for free play. These keep the child interested. At the same time, they are learning and growing.

Our programs are aimed at children between the ages of 3 and 5. Children will enjoy playing with others. They will learn basic math and English skills. Our program helps children start grade school. Think of it as a head start for your child!

Our classes are held at two different times. On weekdays, classes are held from noon to 3 p.m. On weekends, classes are held from 9 to 11 a.m. This gives you a lot of choice as a parent. You can choose the day and time that best suits you.

All parents should consider the Shining Light Day Center. It will give your child the best head start in life. Visit our website today to learn more. You can also call a member of our staff to discuss your child's future. You can also drop in any time to watch a class.

Learning Activity	Details
Storytelling	Children listen to stories being told. They answer questions about the story. Then they help write the ending to the story.
Telling Time	Students learn counting skills by using clocks. They count hours and minutes.
Hide and Seek	Children must find blocks hidden in our outdoor play areas. They race to find all the blocks of their color.
Puppet Show	Children use hand puppets to act out stories. They work in pairs.

1 Read this sentence from the passage.

> **They also develop skills <u>easier</u>.**

Which word means the opposite of <u>easier</u>?

Ⓐ   Simpler

Ⓑ   Harder

Ⓒ   Quicker

Ⓓ   Slower

2 Which two words from the passage have about the same meaning?

Ⓐ   *read, speak*

Ⓑ   *fit, healthy*

Ⓒ   *day, time*

Ⓓ   *learning, school*

3 How is the first paragraph mainly organized?

Ⓐ A problem is described and then a solution is given.

Ⓑ Events are described in the order they occur.

Ⓒ Facts are given to support an argument.

Ⓓ A question is asked and then answered.

4 Read this sentence from the passage.

You can also drop in any time to watch a class.

What do the words "drop in" mean?

Ⓐ Phone

Ⓑ Check

Ⓒ Visit

Ⓓ Watch

5   Look at the web below.

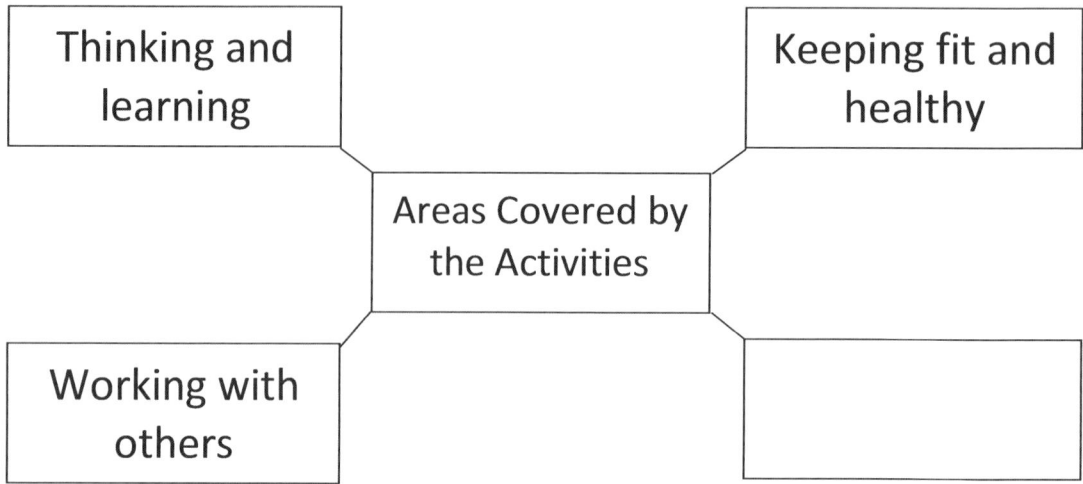

Which of these best completes the web?

- Ⓐ   Reading and speaking
- Ⓑ   Solving problems
- Ⓒ   Understanding shapes
- Ⓓ   Making decisions

6   The passage was probably written mainly to –

- Ⓐ   encourage parents to send their children to the day center
- Ⓑ   compare the day center with grade school
- Ⓒ   describe why the day center was started
- Ⓓ   inform parents about the benefits of learning

7 Which sentence is included mainly to persuade the reader?

   Ⓐ   *As parents, it can be hard to find time for all this.*

   Ⓑ   *Our programs are aimed at children between the ages of 3 and 5.*

   Ⓒ   *On weekdays, classes are held from noon to 3 p.m.*

   Ⓓ   *It will give your child the best head start in life.*

8 Which activity from the table would be most likely to help develop math skills?

   Ⓐ   Storytelling

   Ⓑ   Telling Time

   Ⓒ   Hide and Seek

   Ⓓ   Puppet Show

Section 2
Vocabulary Quizzes

INTRODUCTION TO THE VOCABULARY QUIZZES
For Parents, Teachers, and Tutors

How Vocabulary is Assessed by the State of Texas

The STAAR Reading test includes multiple-choice questions that assess vocabulary skills. These questions follow each passage and are mixed in with the reading comprehension questions.

These questions require students to complete the following tasks:
- identify word meanings
- analyze word meanings in context
- understand and use suffixes
- understand and use prefixes
- understand and use Greek and Latin roots
- identify antonyms (words that have opposite meanings)
- identify synonyms (words that have the same meaning)

About the Vocabulary Quizzes

This section of the practice test book contains six quizzes. Each quiz tests one vocabulary skill that is covered on the state test.

This section of the book covers all of the vocabulary skills assessed on the STAAR Reading test. The aim of the quizzes is to help ensure that students have all the vocabulary skills that they will need for the STAAR Reading test.

If students can master this section of the book, they will be ready to answer the vocabulary questions.

Quiz 1: Identify Word Meanings

1. What does the word <u>ashamed</u> mean in the sentence below?

    Karl felt ashamed of the mess he had made.

    Ⓐ Proud
    Ⓑ Embarrassed
    Ⓒ Worried
    Ⓓ Pleased

2. What does the word <u>entire</u> mean in the sentence below?

    After the storm, the entire yard was covered with snow.

    Ⓐ Whole
    Ⓑ Large
    Ⓒ Cold
    Ⓓ Outside

3. What does the word <u>sink</u> mean in the sentence below?

    The old boat started to sink below the waves.

    Ⓐ To go under
    Ⓑ A bowl or basin
    Ⓒ To become worse
    Ⓓ To dig or drill

Quiz 1: Identify Word Meanings

4 What does the word <u>expert</u> in the sentence below show?

   Josh read many books and became an expert on snakes.

   Ⓐ   Josh knew a lot about snakes.

   Ⓑ   Josh was not afraid of snakes.

   Ⓒ   Josh owned snakes.

   Ⓓ   Josh liked snakes very much.

5 What does the word <u>exchange</u> mean in the sentence below?

   Mandy decided to exchange the dress for another.

   Ⓐ   Make

   Ⓑ   Buy

   Ⓒ   Swap

   Ⓓ   Sell

6 What does the word <u>silent</u> show?

   Carrie was alone in the woods and everything was silent.

   Ⓐ   There was nobody else around.

   Ⓑ   There was no noise.

   Ⓒ   There was very little light.

   Ⓓ   There was a problem.

Quiz 2: Analyze Word Meanings

1. If an object is <u>rocketing</u> through the air, it is —

    Ⓐ   letting off flames

    Ⓑ   traveling upwards

    Ⓒ   spinning around

    Ⓓ   moving very quickly

2. In which sentence does <u>type</u> mean the same as below?

    Kent asked Penny what type of cake she wanted.

    Ⓐ   It took Allan a long time to type the letter.

    Ⓑ   The type on the old newspaper made it hard to read.

    Ⓒ   Anna said that Morgan was not her type.

    Ⓓ   Kyle couldn't decide what type of car to buy.

3. What does the word <u>rose</u> mean in the sentence?

    The people in the crowd rose and started clapping.

    Ⓐ   Stood up

    Ⓑ   Moved higher

    Ⓒ   Developed

    Ⓓ   Puffed up

Quiz 2: Analyze Word Meanings

4 How is <u>shoving</u> a person different from <u>pushing</u> a person?

- Ⓐ The person is pushed over.
- Ⓑ The person is pushed roughly.
- Ⓒ The person is pushed lightly.
- Ⓓ The person is pushed gently.

5 Which word can be used to complete both sentences?

> The summer day was sunny and _____.
> Jacob got a _____ for parking his car on the curb.

- Ⓐ clear
- Ⓑ fine
- Ⓒ warm
- Ⓓ speech

6 Why does the author use the word <u>swooped</u> in the sentence?

> The bird swooped down and picked up the worm.

- Ⓐ To show that the bird looked beautiful
- Ⓑ To show that the bird was flying
- Ⓒ To show that the bird moved quickly downwards
- Ⓓ To show that the bird was clumsy

Quiz 3: Use Synonyms and Antonyms

1. Read the sentence below.

    The road was very slippery when it was wet.

    Which word is closest in meaning to <u>slippery</u>?
    - Ⓐ Greasy
    - Ⓑ Dangerous
    - Ⓒ Damp
    - Ⓓ Shady

2. Which word means about the same as <u>popular</u>?
    - Ⓐ Unusual
    - Ⓑ Well-liked
    - Ⓒ Hated
    - Ⓓ Common

3. Which two words have about the same meaning?
    - Ⓐ Cute, small
    - Ⓑ Peaceful, calm
    - Ⓒ Distant, close
    - Ⓓ Smart, worker

Quiz 3: Use Synonyms and Antonyms

4 Read the sentence below.

> **Hannah said the light color made her room seem dull.**

Which word means the opposite of <u>dull</u>?

- Ⓐ Welcoming
- Ⓑ Boring
- Ⓒ Exciting
- Ⓓ Cold

5 Which word means the opposite of <u>shallow</u>?

- Ⓐ Low
- Ⓑ Thin
- Ⓒ Deep
- Ⓓ Wide

6 Which two words have opposite meanings?

- Ⓐ Pause, wait
- Ⓑ Leap, jump
- Ⓒ Strange, weird
- Ⓓ Firm, soft

Quiz 4: Use Prefixes

1. What does the word <u>reheat</u> mean?

   Ⓐ Heat more

   Ⓑ Not heat

   Ⓒ Heat before

   Ⓓ Heat again

2. Which prefix can be added to the word <u>spell</u> to make a word meaning "spell incorrectly"?

   Ⓐ pre-

   Ⓑ non-

   Ⓒ mis-

   Ⓓ dis-

3. Which prefix should be added to the word to make the sentence correct?

   The dog ___obeyed George and ran off.

   Ⓐ un-

   Ⓑ dis-

   Ⓒ in-

   Ⓓ mis-

Quiz 4: Use Prefixes

4 What does the word <u>nonstop</u> mean?

   Ⓐ   Without stopping

   Ⓑ   Stopping once

   Ⓒ   Stopping often

   Ⓓ   Stopping first

5 Which prefix can be added to the word <u>fair</u> to make a word meaning "not fair"?

   Ⓐ   un-

   Ⓑ   in-

   Ⓒ   mis-

   Ⓓ   dis-

6 Which word means "pay before"?

   Ⓐ   Prepay

   Ⓑ   Repay

   Ⓒ   Mispay

   Ⓓ   Unpay

Quiz 5: Use Suffixes

1. What does the word <u>sweetest</u> mean?
   - Ⓐ Not sweet
   - Ⓑ More sweet
   - Ⓒ The most sweet
   - Ⓓ In a way that is sweet

2. Which suffix can be added to the word <u>fault</u> to make a word meaning "without fault"?
   - Ⓐ -less
   - Ⓑ -ful
   - Ⓒ -ing
   - Ⓓ -ed

3. Which suffix should be added to the word to make the sentence correct?

   The cave was in total dark_____.

   - Ⓐ -ful
   - Ⓑ -est
   - Ⓒ -ness
   - Ⓓ -er

Quiz 5: Use Suffixes

4. What does the word <u>flavorful</u> mean?
   - Ⓐ Having flavor
   - Ⓑ The most flavor
   - Ⓒ The act of flavoring
   - Ⓓ Lacking flavor

5. Which suffix can be added to the word <u>cloud</u> to make a word meaning "full of clouds"?
   - Ⓐ -s
   - Ⓑ -ing
   - Ⓒ -y
   - Ⓓ -ed

6. In which word is the suffix –er used?
   - Ⓐ Reindeer
   - Ⓑ Butler
   - Ⓒ Darker
   - Ⓓ Sister

Quiz 6: Use Greek and Latin Roots

1. The word <u>aquatic</u> contains the Latin root <u>aqua-</u>. An <u>aquatic</u> plant is probably one that —

   Ⓐ lives on land

   Ⓑ lives in water

   Ⓒ needs sunlight

   Ⓓ has flowers

2. The Latin root <u>glaci-</u> is used in the word <u>glacier</u>. What does the Latin root <u>glaci-</u> mean?

   Ⓐ Cold

   Ⓑ Ice

   Ⓒ Far

   Ⓓ Water

3. The word <u>spectator</u> is based on the Latin root <u>spect-</u>, which means "watch or look at." Based on this, what is a <u>spectator</u>?

   Ⓐ Someone who looks good

   Ⓑ Someone who is watching something

   Ⓒ Someone who knows the time

   Ⓓ Someone who wears glasses

Quiz 6: Use Greek and Latin Roots

4 The word <u>monotone</u> contains the Greek root <u>mono-</u>. What does the word <u>monotone</u> mean?

- Ⓐ One tone
- Ⓑ Two tones
- Ⓒ Many tones
- Ⓓ More tones

5 The Greek root <u>oct-</u> is used in the word <u>octopus</u>. What does the Greek root <u>oct-</u> mean?

- Ⓐ Ocean
- Ⓑ Leg
- Ⓒ Eight
- Ⓓ Animal

6 The word <u>multicolored</u> is based on the Latin root <u>multi-</u>, which means "many." Based on this, what does <u>multicolored</u> mean?

- Ⓐ Something that is bright
- Ⓑ Something with more than one color
- Ⓒ Something that is nice to look at
- Ⓓ Something that is shared

Section 3
STAAR Reading Practice Test

INTRODUCTION TO THE READING PRACTICE TEST
For Parents, Teachers, and Tutors

How Reading is Assessed by the State of Texas

The STAAR Reading test assesses reading skills by having students read passages and answer reading comprehension questions about the passages. On the STAAR Reading test, students read 6 to 7 passages and answer a total of 44 multiple-choice questions. Students are given 4 hours to complete the test.

About the STAAR Reading Practice Test

This section of the book contains a practice test just like the real STAAR Reading test. It has 6 passages and a total of 44 multiple-choice questions. The questions cover all the skills tested on the STAAR Reading test, and have the same formats. In short, taking this practice test is just like taking the real STAAR test.

Students are given 4 hours to complete the real STAAR Reading test. You can use the same time limit, or you can choose not to time the test. If using a 4-hour time limit, it is recommended that the student be given a 5 to 10 minute break each hour.

Students complete the STAAR Reading test by marking their answers on an answer sheet. An optional answer sheet is included in the back of the book.

Reading Skills

The STAAR Reading test given by the state of Texas tests a specific set of skills. The full answer key at the end of the book identifies what skill each question is testing.

There are also key reading skills that students will need to understand to master the STAAR Reading test. The answer key includes additional information on these key skills so you can help the student gain understanding.

STAAR Reading

Practice Test

Instructions

Read the passages. Each passage is followed by questions.

Read each question carefully. Then select the best answer. Fill in the circle for the correct answer.

Summer Lemonade

Lemonade is one of the most popular summer drinks in the United States. It is refreshing and helps you to cool down during the hot summer months. Lemonade is available in most stores and can be <u>purchased</u> as a premade drink. These brands are often made with added sugar and other chemicals. These ingredients often make the drink unhealthy. So we're going to make a healthy homemade lemonade!

To make our own lemonade at home we'll need the right ingredients. You will need 1 cup of sugar, 6 lemons, 1 cup of boiling water, and 4 cups of cold water. You will also need a saucepan and a large pitcher.

Step 1

Start by placing the sugar in a saucepan. Then add the boiling water and heat the mixture gently.

Step 2

Extract the juice from your 6 lemons. You can use a juicer. Or you can squeeze them by hand. Add the lemon juice to the water and sugar mixture.

Step 3

Pour the mixture into a pitcher. Then take your 4 cups of cold water and add these to the pitcher. This will cool the mixture down and make it ready to refrigerate. The amount of cold water that you add will affect the strength of the lemonade. You can add more water if you like it <u>weaker</u>.

Step 4

Refrigerate the mixture for 30 or 40 minutes. Taste your lemonade mixture. If it is too sweet, add a little more lemon juice. If it is too strong, add some more water. If it is too sour, add some more sugar.

Step 5

You are now ready to serve your lemonade. Pour it into a glass with ice and a slice of lemon.

1   Read this sentence from the passage.

   Lemonade is available in most stores and can be <u>purchased</u> as a premade drink.

   What does the word <u>purchased</u> mean?

   Ⓐ   Made

   Ⓑ   Found

   Ⓒ   Bought

   Ⓓ   Eaten

2   What would be the best way to improve how the information in paragraph 2 is presented?

   Ⓐ   Add bullet points

   Ⓑ   Add a diagram

   Ⓒ   Add a chart

   Ⓓ   Add a graph

3 What is the main purpose of the passage?

- Ⓐ To instruct
- Ⓑ To entertain
- Ⓒ To inform
- Ⓓ To persuade

4 Read this sentence from the passage.

You can add more water if you like it <u>weaker</u>.

Which word means the opposite of <u>weaker</u>?

- Ⓐ Nicer
- Ⓑ Stronger
- Ⓒ Thinner
- Ⓓ Colder

5   According to the passage, what should you add if the lemonade is too sour?

   Ⓐ   Lemon juice

   Ⓑ   Water

   Ⓒ   Sugar

   Ⓓ   Salt

6   According to the passage, why is homemade lemonade better than lemonade from a store?

   Ⓐ   It lasts longer.

   Ⓑ   It is cheaper.

   Ⓒ   It is better for you.

   Ⓓ   It is easier to make.

7   In which step is the sugar first needed?

   Ⓐ   Step 1

   Ⓑ   Step 2

   Ⓒ   Step 3

   Ⓓ   Step 4

8   What is the main purpose of the first paragraph?

   Ⓐ   To describe how to make lemonade

   Ⓑ   To encourage people to want to make lemonade

   Ⓒ   To tell what lemonade is made from

   Ⓓ   To explain where to get lemonade from

The Taming of the Lion

The lion had a <u>fearful</u> roar
that scared all who dared to follow.
It made his victims run and hide,
and pray for their tomorrow.

His mane was as glorious as sunshine,
and framed his handsome face.
His lair was known to all around
as a truly frightening place.

Until he met a maiden,
and fell hopelessly in love.
His roar became a whisper,
a soft sound to birds above.

His lair was soon a palace,
a kindly home of gentle calm,
where he would hold his loved ones,
and make sure they met no harm.

The lion never harmed another,
or chased his worried prey.
Instead they lived in harmony
and shared each summer's day.

He had been tamed within an instant
by the gentle hand of love,
that would keep his calm forever
beneath the flight of gentle doves.

9 Read this line from the poem.

> **The lion had a <u>fearful</u> roar**

What does the word <u>fearful</u> mean?

- Ⓐ Without fear
- Ⓑ Having fear
- Ⓒ More fear
- Ⓓ Less fear

10 According to the poem, why does the lion become tamer?

- Ⓐ He gets older.
- Ⓑ He falls in love.
- Ⓒ He has children.
- Ⓓ He starts feeling lonely.

11 What is the rhyme pattern of each stanza of the poem?

    Ⓐ   The second and fourth lines rhyme.

    Ⓑ   There are two pairs of rhyming lines.

    Ⓒ   The first and last lines rhyme.

    Ⓓ   None of the lines rhyme.

12 Which line from the poem contains a simile?

    Ⓐ   *His mane was as glorious as sunshine,*

    Ⓑ   *and framed his handsome face.*

    Ⓒ   *His lair was known to all around*

    Ⓓ   *as a truly frightening place.*

13 Which word best describes the tone of the poem?

- Ⓐ Funny
- Ⓑ Serious
- Ⓒ Sweet
- Ⓓ Tense

14 Read this line from the poem.

a soft sound to birds above

Which literary device does the poet use in this line?

- Ⓐ Simile
- Ⓑ Metaphor
- Ⓒ Alliteration
- Ⓓ Personification

15 Read this line from the poem.

He had been tamed within an instant

What does the phrase "within an instant" mean?

Ⓐ   Very well

Ⓑ   Unusually

Ⓒ   Suddenly

Ⓓ   Over a long time

16 Read this line from the poem.

His roar became a whisper,

What does this change show about the lion?

Ⓐ   He has become shy.

Ⓑ   He is no longer scary.

Ⓒ   He feels afraid.

Ⓓ   He listens to others.

Baseball

Baseball is a bat and ball sport that is very popular in America. It is a game played between two teams of nine players. The aim of the game is to score runs. Players <u>strike</u> the ball with a bat. Then they run around four bases. When they cross home base again, they have scored a run. The bases are set at each corner of a 90-foot square called the diamond.

Each team takes it in turns to bat while the other fields. The other team must stop the batters from scoring runs by getting them out. To get a batter out, they can strike them out. This means that the batter misses the ball three times. They can also get them out by catching the ball if the batter isn't safe on a base. Players can stop at any of the four bases once they have hit the ball, which makes them safe.

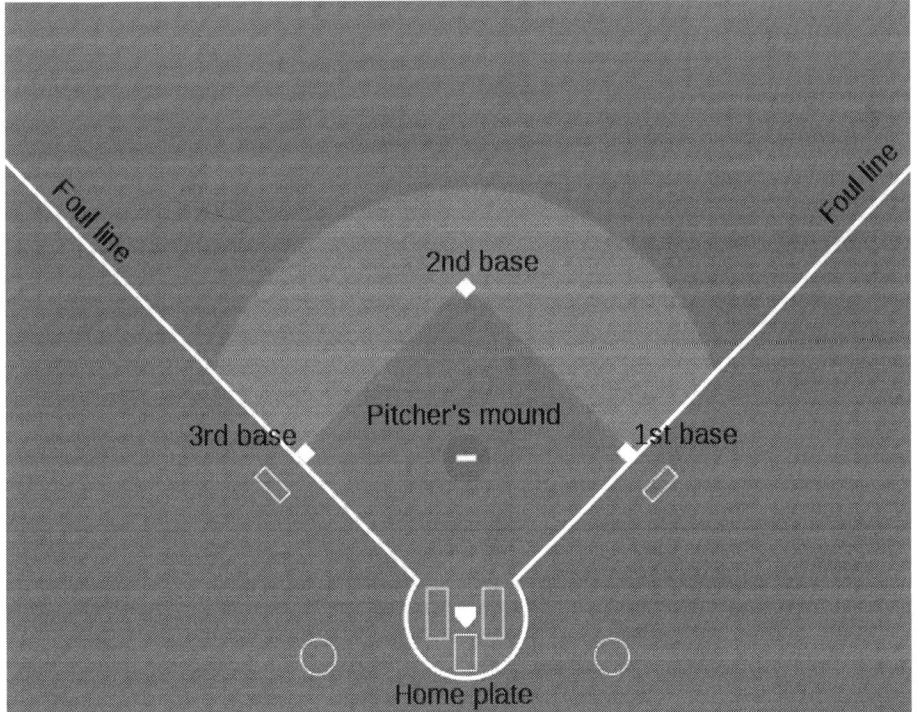

Once three players are out, the fielding team takes their turn to bat. Each time a team bats, it is known as an innings. There are nine innings in a professional league game. The team that scores the most runs at the close of all innings is the winner. The player who throws the ball to the batting team is known as the pitcher. Each professional game has two umpires who ensure <u>fair</u> play between the teams. They judge whether players on the batting team are out or not. Umpires also decide whether or not pitchers throw the ball correctly.

Baseball developed from the traditional bat and ball games of the 18th century. It has a sister sport referred to as rounders. Both of these sports were first played in America by British and Irish immigrants. It has since developed to become known as the national sport of North America. Over the last 20 years, the sport has also grown worldwide. It is now very popular in the Caribbean, South America, and many parts of Asia.

Baseball is a great sport for young kids. It is safer than contact sports like football. It requires a range of skills. Players can focus on being good batters, pitchers, or fielders. At the same time, players learn to work together as a team.

17 Read this sentence from the passage.

> **Each professional game has two umpires who ensure <u>fair</u> play between the teams.**

Which meaning of the word <u>fair</u> is used in this sentence?

- Ⓐ Average
- Ⓑ Just or correct
- Ⓒ Pale
- Ⓓ Sunny or clear

18 What is the player who throws the ball to the batting team called?

- Ⓐ Bowler
- Ⓑ Runner
- Ⓒ Catcher
- Ⓓ Pitcher

19 Which sentence from the passage is an opinion?

   Ⓐ   *It is a game played between two teams of nine players.*

   Ⓑ   *Each time a team bats, it is known as an innings.*

   Ⓒ   *Over the last 20 years, the sport has also grown worldwide.*

   Ⓓ   *It is safer than contact sports like football.*

20 What does the diagram most help the reader understand?

   Ⓐ   How many players are on a team

   Ⓑ   The main rules of baseball

   Ⓒ   Where the bases are located

   Ⓓ   What the purpose of the pitcher is

21 According to the passage, which of these is NOT a term related to baseball?

- Ⓐ Diamond
- Ⓑ Platform
- Ⓒ Strike
- Ⓓ Innings

22 The passage was probably written mainly to –

- Ⓐ encourage people to play sport
- Ⓑ teach readers about the sport of baseball
- Ⓒ show why baseball is popular
- Ⓓ describe the history of baseball

23 Read this sentence from the passage.

Players strike the ball with a bat.

Which word could best be used in place of strike?

Ⓐ Swap

Ⓑ Shove

Ⓒ Hit

Ⓓ Throw

A Special Day

Dear Diary,

Today was quite an amazing day for me. It was the day that my father returned home from overseas. He had been away from us for over a year. We had missed him more than words could ever say. Although we were proud of him, we longed for the day when he would wake up under the same roof as us. Now the day had finally arrived. He had worked hard and it was now time for him to return home.

Mom woke us at 6 a.m. to head to the airport. My father's flight was due in at 9:30. "We don't want to be late!" she kept saying as she woke everyone up. She had no need to remind me! I quickly dressed, washed, and made my way downstairs for breakfast. I could not take my eyes off the clock all morning. Time was going so slowly. When the clock struck 8:45, my mom told us all it was time to go. We all raced to the car and made our way quickly to the airport.

We arrived just after 9 and hurried to the terminal to wait patiently. But 9:30 came and went and our father's flight had still not arrived. Another 10 minutes went by, and I started pacing up and down. I kept asking Mom where he was. She just kept smiling and saying he'd be there soon. Suddenly a gap appeared in the crowd and a tall shadow emerged. There was my father standing before me. He dropped his bags to the floor and swept my sister and I up in his arms. "I've missed you so much," he said through tears of joy. We all cried together. I never want my father to ever let me go.

Today was pretty perfect.

Holly

24 Read this sentence from the letter.

> **We had missed him more than words could ever say.**

Which literary device is used in this sentence?

- Ⓐ Imagery, using details to create an image or picture
- Ⓑ Hyperbole, using exaggeration to make a point
- Ⓒ Simile, comparing two items using the words "like" or "as"
- Ⓓ Symbolism, using an object to stand for something else

25 Read this sentence from the letter.

> **I could not take my eyes off the clock all morning.**

This sentence shows that Holly was –

- Ⓐ worried
- Ⓑ excited
- Ⓒ bored
- Ⓓ patient

26 Why does Holly most likely say that she doesn't need to be reminded not to be late?

- Ⓐ She does not care if they are late.
- Ⓑ She knows that the plane will be late.
- Ⓒ She would never want to be late.
- Ⓓ She thinks that they will be late anyway.

27 How is the second paragraph mainly organized?

- Ⓐ A problem is described and then a solution is given.
- Ⓑ Events are described in the order they occur.
- Ⓒ Facts are given to support an argument.
- Ⓓ A question is asked and then answered.

28 The reader can tell that Holly's father –

- Ⓐ missed his family very much
- Ⓑ wants to go overseas again
- Ⓒ is surprised to be home
- Ⓓ thinks his kids have grown up a lot

29 How does Holly most likely feel while waiting at the airport?

- Ⓐ   Surprised
- Ⓑ   Anxious
- Ⓒ   Calm
- Ⓓ   Bored

30 Which sentence from the letter best shows how Holly feels about having her father home?

- Ⓐ   *There was my father standing before me.*
- Ⓑ   *He dropped his bags to the floor and swept my sister and I up in his arms.*
- Ⓒ   *We all cried together.*
- Ⓓ   *I never want my father to ever let me go.*

Share and Share Alike

Thomas could be quite mean at times. He had a younger brother called Simon and he <u>rarely</u> shared his toys with him.

"You must share Thomas," urged his mother. "One day you will want somebody to share something with you and they won't. Then you will be very upset."

Thomas just laughed his mother's advice off.

"I'll be fine, Mom," he replied. "As long as I have my own toys, I will always be fine."

His mother just shrugged her shoulders.

"Very well," she said. "It seems that you know best."

One day she decided to teach him a lesson. At Christmas, she knew that both boys wanted the same video game. She also knew that if she bought it for Thomas, Simon would never get to play it. So she purchased the game to give to Simon.

When Christmas day arrived, both boys were patiently waiting for their presents in front of the fireplace. As Simon <u>tore</u> into the video game package, his eyes lit up. Thomas saw it was the game he wanted and grinned.

"Thank you so much!" Simon said.

"There is just one thing, Simon," Simon's mother said. "You cannot share this game with your brother."

Thomas's smiled turned quickly into a frown.

"Why not, Mom?" Thomas asked gruffly.

"Because you fail to share any of your toys with Simon and it wouldn't be fair," his mother replied. "If you did share some of your toys with Simon, then I am sure he will let you play his game."

Thomas paused and thought for a moment.

"Okay," he whispered quietly, "that seems fair."

From that day on, the two boys shared all their toys and games.

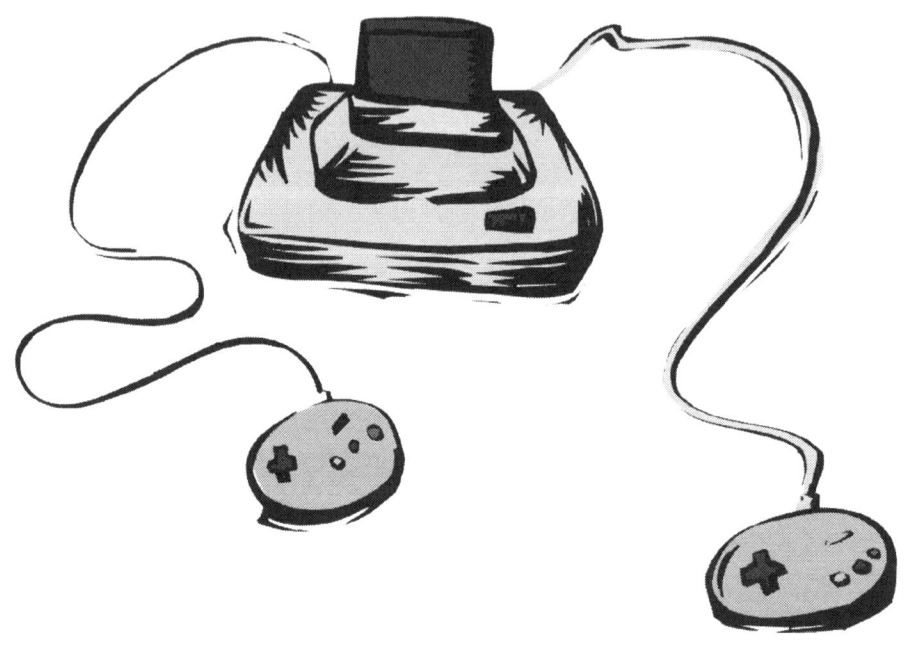

31 Read this sentence from the passage.

> **He had a younger brother called Simon and he <u>rarely</u> shared his toys with him.**

Which word means the opposite of <u>rarely</u>?

- Ⓐ Sometimes
- Ⓑ Never
- Ⓒ Often
- Ⓓ Once

32 Read this sentence from the passage.

> **As Simon <u>tore</u> into the video game package, his eyes lit up.**

The word <u>tore</u> suggests that Simon opened the package –

- Ⓐ slowly
- Ⓑ roughly
- Ⓒ carefully
- Ⓓ calmly

33 According to the passage, how is Simon different from Thomas?

- Ⓐ He is selfish.
- Ⓑ He is younger.
- Ⓒ He is kinder.
- Ⓓ He is wiser.

34 Who is telling the story?

- Ⓐ Simon
- Ⓑ Thomas
- Ⓒ Thomas's mother
- Ⓓ Someone not in the story

35 Why does Thomas most likely grin when he sees the video game?

- Ⓐ He knows that Simon wanted it.
- Ⓑ He doesn't want to show that he is upset.
- Ⓒ He thinks that he will be able to play it.
- Ⓓ He expects his present to be the same.

36 Where would this passage most likely be found?

- Ⓐ In a book of poems
- Ⓑ In a magazine
- Ⓒ In a science textbook
- Ⓓ In a book of short stories

37 The main theme of the passage is about –

- Ⓐ getting along with your siblings
- Ⓑ sharing your things with others
- Ⓒ buying good presents
- Ⓓ thinking of clever plans

The King's Choice

The King lived in a grand hillside castle. He had riches and wealth beyond the dreams of his subjects. He had all the time in the world to enjoy them. There was just one thing missing from his life. He longed to find love and a partner for life.

His search had led him thousands of miles across the world. He had been through Europe, America, and all over Asia. He had searched everywhere for a queen. He was finally about to give up. Then one day a poor man arrived at his court with his daughter.

The poor man had heard of the King's troubles. He made him an offer. He would allow his daughter to become the King's wife for a fee. His daughter's name was Abigail. When the King saw her, he fell in love straight away.

"I am in love with your daughter," he declared boldly. "I would like to marry her tomorrow. I will give you all of the riches that you desire."

The poor man paused and whispered quietly.

"Good King, all I require for the hand of my daughter is your entire empire. I want all of your money, riches, and castles. I want to be the king of this land. In return, you will have a wife."

The King was shocked. He hadn't expected that he would have to give up everything. He would no longer be king and he would have to live his life as a poor man. Yet as he looked into the eyes of Abigail, it was a <u>simple</u> decision.

"Sir, I accept your offer," he declared. "I will give everything I own for your daughter's hand in marriage."

He handed the poor man his crown. He took Abigail into his arms and kissed her cheek. Within hours, they were married. He was never rich or powerful again. However, he never regretted his decision. He and his new wife lived a happy life together until the end of time.

38 Read this sentence from the passage.

> **The King lived in a <u>grand</u> hillside castle.**

What does the word <u>grand</u> mean?

Ⓐ   Large

Ⓑ   Strange

Ⓒ   Old

Ⓓ   Tiny

39 Read this sentence from the passage.

> **Yet as he looked into the eyes of Abigail, it was a <u>simple</u> decision.**

As it is used in this sentence, what does the word <u>simple</u> mean?

Ⓐ   Difficult

Ⓑ   Easy

Ⓒ   Silly

Ⓓ   Fast

40 What type of passage is "The King's Choice"?

- Ⓐ Short story
- Ⓑ Science fiction story
- Ⓒ Letter
- Ⓓ Fable

41 What is the main purpose of the first paragraph?

- Ⓐ To describe the setting of the passage
- Ⓑ To describe the King's main problem
- Ⓒ To compare the King to the poor man
- Ⓓ To suggest that the King makes the wrong choice

42 What happens right after the King sees Abigail for the first time?

- Ⓐ He decides to travel the world.
- Ⓑ He says he wants to marry her.
- Ⓒ He goes to visit the poor man.
- Ⓓ He throws his crown away.

43 Which of these best describes the theme of the passage?

  Ⓐ   It is important to take a chance sometimes.

  Ⓑ   There are more important things in life than money.

  Ⓒ   Good things come to those who wait.

  Ⓓ   People who work hard will be rewarded.

44 What is the point of view in the passage?

  Ⓐ   First person

  Ⓑ   Second person

  Ⓒ   Third person limited

  Ⓓ   Third person omniscient

END OF TEST

Answer Key

The STAAR Reading test given by the state of Texas assesses a specific set of skills. The answer key identifies what skill each question is testing.

The answer key also includes notes on key reading skills that students will need to understand to master the test. Use the notes to review the questions with students so they gain a full understanding of these key reading skills.

Section 1: Reading Mini-Tests

Mini-Test 1

The Change

Question	Answer	Reading Skill
1	C	Use prefixes and suffixes to determine the meaning of a word*
2	B	Identify and use antonyms
3	C	Identify the main character
4	B	Understand and analyze word use
5	D	Identify point of view*
6	A	Identify the main problem in a passage
7	B	Identify the sequence of events
8	D	Identify and summarize the theme of a passage

*Key Reading Skill: Prefixes and Suffixes

A prefix is a word part that is placed at the start of a word, such as *un-* or *dis-*. The word *insecure* is the base word *secure* with the prefix *in-* added to the start. The meaning of *insecure* is "not secure or not confident."

*Key Reading Skill: Point of View

This question is asking about the point of view of the passage. There are three main points of view. They are:

- First person – the story is told by a narrator who is a character in the story. The use of the words *I*, *my*, or *we* indicate a first person point of view. *Example: I went for a hike. After a while, my legs began to ache.*
- Second person – the story is told by referring to the reader as "you." *Example: You are hiking. After a while, your legs begin to ache.*
- Third person – the story is told by a person outside the story. *Example: Jacky went for a hike. After a while, her legs began to ache.*

The story has a third person point of view. It is told by someone who is not in the story.

Mini-Test 2

Muhammad Ali

Question	Answer	Reading Skill
1	D	Use context to determine the meaning of words
2	C	Use prefixes and suffixes to determine the meaning of a word*
3	A	Locate facts and details in a passage
4	A	Identify different types of texts*
5	B	Distinguish between important and unimportant details
6	D	Distinguish between fact and opinion*
7	A	Identify details that support a conclusion
8	B	Identify how a passage is organized*

*Key Reading Skill: Prefixes and Suffixes

A prefix is a word part that is placed at the start of a word, such as *un-* or *dis-*. The word *reclaimed* is the base word *claimed* with the prefix *re-* added to the start. The meaning of *reclaimed* is "claimed again."

*Key Reading Skill: Identifying Genres (Biography)

A biography is a story of someone's life written by someone other than the person described. This is different to an autobiography, which is the story of someone's life written by that person.

*Key Reading Skill: Fact and Opinion

A fact is a statement that can be proven to be correct. An opinion is a statement that cannot be proven to be correct. An opinion is what somebody thinks about something. The sentence given in answer choice D is an opinion. The other sentences are facts.

*Key Reading Skill: Patterns of Organization

There are several common ways that passages are organized. Students will often be asked to identify how a passage, or a paragraph within a passage, is organized. The common patterns of organization are:

- Cause and effect – a cause of something is described and then its effect is described
- Chronological order, or sequence of events – events are described in the order that they occurred
- Compare and contrast – two or more people, events, places, or objects are compared or contrasted
- Problem and solution – a problem is described and then a solution to the problem is given
- Main idea/supporting details – a main idea is stated and then details are given to support the main idea
- Question and answer – a question is asked and then answered

Mini-Test 3

Little Things

Question	Answer	Reading Skill
1	B	Use context to determine the meaning of words
2	C	Understand and analyze word use
3	D	Identify the mood of a passage*
4	A	Understand and analyze literary techniques (alliteration)*
5	C	Identify the characteristics of poems
6	A	Understand and analyze literary techniques (repetition)
7	A	Identify and summarize the theme of a passage
8	C	Identify the main idea

*Key Reading Skill: Mood

The mood of a passage is the way the passage makes the reader feel. It is the atmosphere of the passage.

*Key Reading Skill: Alliteration

Alliteration is a literary technique where consonant sounds are repeated in neighboring words. This line uses alliteration because of the repeated "m" sound.

Mini-Test 4

Grooming a King Charles Cavalier

Question	Answer	Reading Skill
1	C	Identify and use antonyms
2	B	Use context to determine the meaning of words
3	C	Locate facts and details
4	A	Identify the author's main purpose
5	C	Understand the purpose of text features
6	B	Understand written directions
7	C	Understand and analyze illustrations and photographs
8	B	Identify the sequence of events

Mini-Test 5

The Girlfriend and the Mother

Question	Answer	Reading Skill
1	C	Use context to determine the meaning of words
2	B	Use words with multiple meanings*
3	B	Identify the main problem in a passage
4	D	Identify different types of texts*
5	B	Compare and contrast based on information in a passage
6	B	Identify how characters change
7	C	Identify facts and details
8	B	Make predictions about characters

*Key Reading Skill: Multiple Meanings

Some words have more than one meaning. These words are known as homonyms. All the answer choices are possible meanings for the word *bond*. The correct answer is the one that states the meaning of the word *bond* as it is used in the sentence.

*Key Reading Skill: Identifying Genres (Fable)

A fable is a story that is mainly written to teach a lesson. Fables usually have a moral lesson. Fables usually involve characters that are animals, elements of nature such as wind or the Sun, or royal characters such as kings, queens, and princes.

Mini-Test 6

Moving On

Question	Answer	Reading Skill
1	D	Identify and use synonyms
2	B	Use words with multiple meanings*
3	C	Locate facts and details in a passage
4	B	Identify the author's main purpose
5	A	Understand cause and effect
6	B	Identify the meaning of phrases
7	D	Identify details that support a conclusion
8	C	Make inferences based on information in a passage

*Key Reading Skill: Multiple Meanings

Some words have more than one meaning. These words are known as homonyms. All the answer choices are possible meanings for the word *position*. The correct answer is the one that states the meaning of the word *position* as it is used in the sentence.

Mini-Test 7

Catching Up

Question	Answer	Reading Skill
1	B	Identify and use synonyms
2	D	Use context to determine the meaning of words
3	A	Identify the meaning of phrases
4	A	Identify the main idea
5	B	Draw conclusions about characters
6	B	Make inferences about characters
7	A	Make inferences based on information in a passage
8	C	Identify different types of texts

Mini-Test 8

The Shining Light Day Center

Question	Answer	Reading Skill
1	B	Identify and use antonyms
2	B	Identify and use synonyms
3	A	Identify how a passage is organized*
4	C	Identify the meaning of phrases
5	A	Summarize information given in a passage
6	A	Identify the author's main purpose
7	D	Identify the purpose of specific information
8	B	Understand information in graphs, charts, or tables

*Key Reading Skill: Patterns of Organization

There are several common ways that passages are organized. Students will often be asked to identify how a passage, or a paragraph within a passage, is organized. The common patterns of organization are:

- Cause and effect – a cause of something is described and then its effect is described
- Chronological order, or sequence of events – events are described in the order that they occurred
- Compare and contrast – two or more people, events, places, or objects are compared or contrasted
- Problem and solution – a problem is described and then a solution to the problem is given
- Main idea/supporting details – a main idea is stated and then details are given to support the main idea
- Question and answer – a question is asked and then answered

Section 2: Vocabulary Quizzes

Quiz 1: Identify Word Meanings

Question	Answer
1	B
2	A
3	A
4	A
5	C
6	B

Quiz 2: Analyze Word Meanings

Question	Answer
1	D
2	D
3	A
4	B
5	B
6	C

Quiz 3: Use Synonyms and Antonyms

Question	Answer
1	A
2	B
3	B
4	C
5	C
6	D

Quiz 4: Use Prefixes

Question	Answer
1	D
2	C
3	B
4	A
5	A
6	A

Quiz 5: Use Suffixes

Question	Answer
1	C
2	A
3	C
4	A
5	C
6	C

Quiz 6: Use Greek and Latin Roots

Question	Answer
1	B
2	B
3	B
4	A
5	C
6	B

Section 3: STAAR Reading Practice Test

Question	Answer	Reading Skill
1	C	Use context to determine the meaning of words
2	A	Understand the use of text features
3	A	Identify the author's main purpose
4	B	Identify and use antonyms
5	C	Understand written directions
6	C	Locate facts and details in a passage
7	A	Understand written directions
8	B	Identify the author's main purpose
9	B	Use prefixes and suffixes to determine the meaning of a word*
10	B	Understand cause and effect
11	A	Identify the characteristics of poems
12	A	Understand and analyze literary techniques (simile)*
13	C	Identify the tone of a passage*
14	C	Understand and analyze literary techniques (alliteration)*
15	C	Identify the meaning of phrases
16	B	Draw conclusions about characters
17	B	Use words with multiple meanings*
18	D	Locate facts and details in a passage
19	D	Distinguish between fact and opinion*
20	C	Analyze the use of features such as maps, graphs, and diagrams
21	B	Locate facts and details in a passage
22	B	Identify the author's main purpose
23	C	Identify and use synonyms
24	B	Understand and analyze literary techniques (hyperbole)*
25	B	Identify the purpose of specific information
26	C	Make inferences about characters
27	B	Identify how a passage is organized*
28	A	Make inferences based on information in a passage
29	B	Draw conclusions about characters
30	D	Identify details that support a conclusion
31	C	Identify and use antonyms
32	B	Understand and analyze word use
33	B	Compare and contrast based on information in a passage
34	D	Identify point of view*
35	C	Make inferences based on information in a passage
36	D	Identify different types of texts
37	B	Identify and summarize the theme of a passage
38	A	Use context to determine the meaning of words
39	B	Use context to determine the meaning of words
40	D	Identify different types of texts*

41	B	Understand and analyze the plot of a passage
42	B	Identify the sequence of events
43	B	Identify and summarize the theme of a passage
44	D	Identify point of view*

*Key Reading Skills

Q9: Prefixes and Suffixes

A prefix is a word part that is placed at the start of a word, such as *un-* or *dis-*. A suffix is a word part that is placed at the end of a word, such as *-less* or *-ly*.

Q12: Simile

A simile compares two things using the words "like" or "as." The phrase "as glorious as sunshine" is an example of a simile.

Q13: Tone

The tone of a passage refers to the author's attitude. It is how the author feels about the content of the passage. For example, the tone could be playful, sad, cheerful, or witty. In this case, the tone is sweet.

Q14: Alliteration

Alliteration is a literary technique where consonant sounds are repeated in neighboring words. The phrase "soft sound" uses alliteration because of the repeated "s" sound.

Q17: Multiple Meanings

Some words have more than one meaning. These words are known as homonyms. All the answer choices are possible meanings for the word *fair*. The correct answer is the one that states the meaning of the word *fair* as it is used in the sentence.

Q19: Fact and Opinion

A fact is a statement that can be proven to be correct. An opinion is a statement that cannot be proven to be correct. An opinion is what somebody thinks about something. The sentence given in answer choice D is an opinion. It describes what the author thinks and cannot be proven to be true.

Q24: Hyperbole

Hyperbole is a literary technique where exaggeration is used to make a point. The phrase "more than words could ever say" is an example of hyperbole.

Q27: Patterns of Organization

There are several common ways that passages are organized. Students will often be asked to identify how a passage, or a paragraph within a passage, is organized. The common patterns of organization are:

- Cause and effect – a cause of something is described and then its effect is described
- Chronological order, or sequence of events – events are described in the order that they occurred
- Compare and contrast – two or more people, events, places, or objects are compared or contrasted
- Problem and solution – a problem is described and then a solution to the problem is given
- Main idea/supporting details – a main idea is stated and then details are given to support the main idea
- Question and answer – a question is asked and then answered

Q34: Point of View

This question is asking about the point of view of the passage. There are three main points of view. They are:

- First person – the story is told by a narrator who is a character in the story. The use of the words *I*, *my*, or *we* indicate a first person point of view. *Example: I went for a hike. After a while, my legs began to ache.*
- Second person – the story is told by referring to the reader as "you." *Example: You are hiking. After a while, your legs begin to ache.*
- Third person – the story is told by a person outside the story. *Example: Jacky went for a hike. After a while, her legs began to ache.*

The story has a third person point of view. It is told by someone who is not in the story.

Q40: Identifying Genres (Fable)

A fable is a story that is mainly written to teach a lesson. Fables usually have a moral lesson. Fables usually involve characters that are animals, elements of nature such as wind or the Sun, or royal characters such as kings, queens, and princes.

Q44: Point of View

This question is asking about the point of view of the passage. There are four possible points of view. They are:
- First person – the story is told by a narrator who is a character in the story. The use of the words *I*, *my*, or *we* indicate a first person point of view.
  Example: I went for a hike in the mountains. After a while, my legs began to ache.
- Second person – the story is told by referring to the reader as "you." This point of view is rarely used.
  Example: You are hiking in the mountains. After a while, your legs begin to ache.
- Third person limited – the story is told by a person outside the story. The term *limited* refers to how much knowledge the narrator has. The narrator has knowledge of one character, but does not have knowledge beyond what that one character knows, sees, or does.
  Example: Jacky went for a hike in the mountains. After a while, her legs began to ache.
- Third person omniscient – the story is told by a person outside the story. The term *omniscient* refers to how much knowledge the narrator has. An omniscient narrator knows everything about all characters and has unlimited information.
  Example: Jacky went for a hike in the mountains. Like most of the other hikers, her legs began to ache.

The story is told by a person outside the story. The person knows everything about the characters, such as how the King feels and what the King thinks. The point of view of the passage is third person omniscient.

Texas Test Prep Reading Workbook

For additional reading test prep, get the Texas Test Prep Reading Workbook. It contains 40 reading mini-tests covering all the reading skills on the STAAR test. It is the perfect tool for ongoing test prep practice and for reading skills revision.

TEXAS TEST PREP MATH

Help with the Texas STAAR tests is also available for math!

- Powerful up-to-date test prep for the STAAR Math test
- Practice Test Book and Student Quiz Book available
- Covers every math skill needed by Texas students
- Books available from Grades 3 through to 8

MULTIPLE CHOICE ANSWER SHEET

STAAR Reading Practice Test

#		#		#	
1	Ⓐ Ⓑ Ⓒ Ⓓ	16	Ⓐ Ⓑ Ⓒ Ⓓ	31	Ⓐ Ⓑ Ⓒ Ⓓ
2	Ⓐ Ⓑ Ⓒ Ⓓ	17	Ⓐ Ⓑ Ⓒ Ⓓ	32	Ⓐ Ⓑ Ⓒ Ⓓ
3	Ⓐ Ⓑ Ⓒ Ⓓ	18	Ⓐ Ⓑ Ⓒ Ⓓ	33	Ⓐ Ⓑ Ⓒ Ⓓ
4	Ⓐ Ⓑ Ⓒ Ⓓ	19	Ⓐ Ⓑ Ⓒ Ⓓ	34	Ⓐ Ⓑ Ⓒ Ⓓ
5	Ⓐ Ⓑ Ⓒ Ⓓ	20	Ⓐ Ⓑ Ⓒ Ⓓ	35	Ⓐ Ⓑ Ⓒ Ⓓ
6	Ⓐ Ⓑ Ⓒ Ⓓ	21	Ⓐ Ⓑ Ⓒ Ⓓ	36	Ⓐ Ⓑ Ⓒ Ⓓ
7	Ⓐ Ⓑ Ⓒ Ⓓ	22	Ⓐ Ⓑ Ⓒ Ⓓ	37	Ⓐ Ⓑ Ⓒ Ⓓ
8	Ⓐ Ⓑ Ⓒ Ⓓ	23	Ⓐ Ⓑ Ⓒ Ⓓ	38	Ⓐ Ⓑ Ⓒ Ⓓ
9	Ⓐ Ⓑ Ⓒ Ⓓ	24	Ⓐ Ⓑ Ⓒ Ⓓ	39	Ⓐ Ⓑ Ⓒ Ⓓ
10	Ⓐ Ⓑ Ⓒ Ⓓ	25	Ⓐ Ⓑ Ⓒ Ⓓ	40	Ⓐ Ⓑ Ⓒ Ⓓ
11	Ⓐ Ⓑ Ⓒ Ⓓ	26	Ⓐ Ⓑ Ⓒ Ⓓ	41	Ⓐ Ⓑ Ⓒ Ⓓ
12	Ⓐ Ⓑ Ⓒ Ⓓ	27	Ⓐ Ⓑ Ⓒ Ⓓ	42	Ⓐ Ⓑ Ⓒ Ⓓ
13	Ⓐ Ⓑ Ⓒ Ⓓ	28	Ⓐ Ⓑ Ⓒ Ⓓ	43	Ⓐ Ⓑ Ⓒ Ⓓ
14	Ⓐ Ⓑ Ⓒ Ⓓ	29	Ⓐ Ⓑ Ⓒ Ⓓ	44	Ⓐ Ⓑ Ⓒ Ⓓ
15	Ⓐ Ⓑ Ⓒ Ⓓ	30	Ⓐ Ⓑ Ⓒ Ⓓ		

Made in the USA
Lexington, KY
18 February 2012